NOV 2 1 2018

BLUE BANNER
BIOGRAPHY

Carson WENTZ

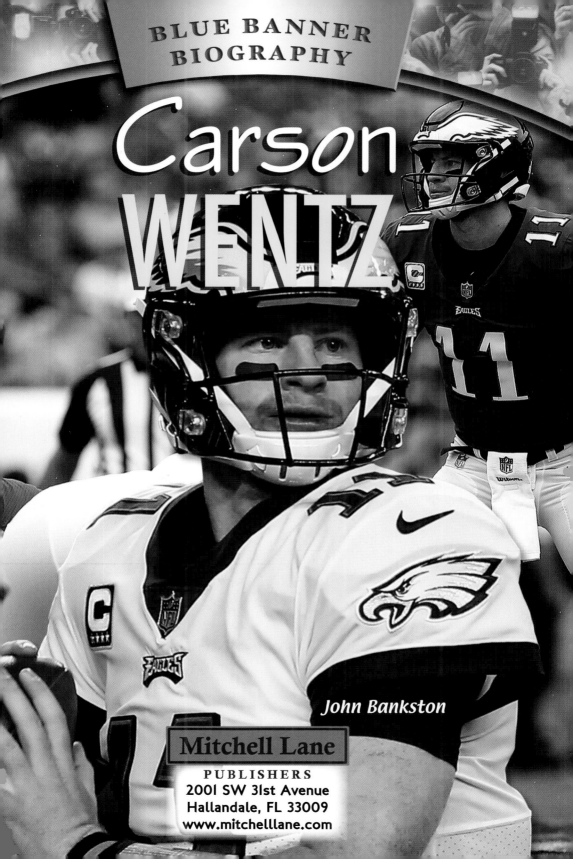

John Bankston

Mitchell Lane

PUBLISHERS
2001 SW 31st Avenue
Hallandale, FL 33009
www.mitchelllane.com

Mitchell Lane
PUBLISHERS

Printing   1   2   3   4   5   6   7   8   9

Blue Banner Biographies

5 Seconds of Summer	Gwen Stefani	Mary-Kate and Ashley Olsen
Aaron Judge	Hope Solo	Megan Fox
Abby Wambach	Ice Cube	Miguel Tejada
Adele	Jamie Foxx	Mike Trout
Alicia Keys	James Harden	Nancy Pelosi
Allen Iverson	Jared Goff	Natasha Bedingfield
Ashanti	Ja Rule	Nicki Minaj
Ashlee Simpson	Jason Derulo	One Direction
Ashton Kutcher	Jay-Z	Orianthi
Avril Lavigne	Jennifer Hudson	Orlando Bloom
Blake Lively	Jennifer Lopez	P. Diddy
Blake Shelton	Jessica Simpson	Peyton Manning
Bow Wow	JJ Watt	Pharrell Williams
Brett Favre	J. K. Rowling	Pit Bull
Britney Spears	John Legend	Prince William
CC Sabathia	Justin Berfield	Queen Latifah
Carrie Underwood	Justin Timberlake	Robert Downey Jr.
Carson Wentz	Kanye West	Ron Howard
Charlie Puth	Kate Hudson	Russell Westbrook
Chris Brown	Keith Urban	Russell Wilson
Chris Daughtry	Kelly Clarkson	Sean Kingston
Christina Aguilera	Kenny Chesney	Selena
Clay Aiken	Ke$ha	Shia LaBeouf
Cole Hamels	Kevin Durant	Shontelle Layne
Condoleezza Rice	Kristen Stewart	Soulja Boy Tell 'Em
Corbin Bleu	Lady Gaga	Stephenie Meyer
Daniel Radcliffe	Lance Armstrong	Taylor Swift
David Ortiz	Leona Lewis	T.I.
David Wright	Le'Veon Bell	Timbaland
Derek Hough	Lindsay Lohan	Tim McGraw
Derek Jeter	LL Cool J	Toby Keith
Drew Brees	Ludacris	Usher
Dwyane Wade	Luke Bryan	Vanessa Anne Hudgens
Eminem	Maren Morris	The Weeknd
Eve	Mariah Carey	Will.i.am
Fergie	Mario	Zac Efron
Flo Rida	Mary J. Blige	

Library of Congress Cataloging-in-Publication Data
Names: Bankston, John, 1974- author.
Title: Carson Wentz / By John Bankston.
Description: Hallandale, FL : Mitchell Lane Publishers, [2019] | Series: Blue banner biographies |
    Includes bibliographical references and index. | Audience: Age 9-13.
Identifiers: LCCN 2018007997 | ISBN 9781680202847 (library bound) | ISBN: 9781680202854 (ebook)
Subjects: LCSH: Wentz, Carson, 1992– —Juvenile literature. | Football players—United States—
    Biography—Juvenile literature.
Classification: LCC GV939.W369 B36 2018 | DDC 796.332092 [B] —dc23
LC record available at https://lccn.loc.gov/2018007997

ABOUT THE AUTHOR: Born in Boston, Massachusetts, John Bankston began writing professionally while still a teenager. Since then, more than 200 of his articles have been published in magazines and newspapers across the country. He is the author of more than 100 nonfiction books for children and young adults, including Mitchell Lane biographies of Abby Wambach, Kevin Durant and Selena Gomez. Today he lives in coastal Florida.

PUBLISHER'S NOTE: The following story has been thoroughly researched and to the best of our knowledge represents a true story. While every possible effort has been made to ensure accuracy, the publisher will not assume liability for damages caused by inaccuracies in the data and makes no warranty on the accuracy of the information contained herein. This story has not been authorized or endorsed by Carson Wentz.

Blue Banner Biography

Carson Wentz prepares to hand off the football during the 2015 FCS National Championship Game. Wentz's North Dakota State Bison defeated Jacksonville State for its fifth straight national title.

1 Game Changer

The North Dakota State University football team has a long tradition of winning. The Bison have won 14 national championships and 34 conference championships. They play in Division I, the top level in college sports. Division I is divided into the Football Bowl Subdivision (FBS) and the Football Championship Subdivision (FCS). The Bison compete in the FCS, against teams like Mississippi Valley State, Missouri State, South Dakota State, and South Dakota. They are not as well-known as FBS teams like Notre Dame, Alabama, and Michigan.

Bison quarterback Carson Wentz was doing his best to live up to the team's lofty standards. On October 17, 2015, North Dakota State was playing the University of South Dakota Coyotes. As the last seconds ticked off, the Coyotes' Miles Bergner made a 33-yard field goal. The final score was 24-21. South Dakota had won.

Losing wasn't the worst thing for Carson that day. He hurt his right wrist. Despite the injury, he completed two touchdown passes. The next day, his wrist was very swollen. He hoped it was a sprain. X-rays revealed the truth. It was broken. He'd injured his throwing arm. After surgery, it would take two months to heal.

Carson was a senior. There was only one way he'd play college football again. The Bison needed to reach the playoffs.

Carson spent time with the new starting quarterback, freshman Easton Stick. Stick had played very little. As Carson later told *Sports Illustrated*, he joked, "No pressure. You only have my college career in your hands."

Growing up, Carson wanted to be a pro football player. Across the country, countless numbers of youngsters have the same dream.

Growing up, Carson wanted to be a pro football player. Across the country, countless numbers of youngsters have the same dream. Not many realize it.

Every February, over 300 of the best college players travel to Indianapolis, Indiana for the NFL (National Football League) Scouting Combine. For four days, they compete in a variety of events. They do bench presses and 40-yard dashes. They jump and they do drills. All 32 NFL teams comb through the results to decide which players they want to pick in the NFL

Draft later that spring. About 250 are drafted. Others sign with teams as free agents. The rest must discover different dreams.

After Carson's injury, many people told him to forget about college ball. They wanted him to focus on the Combine. Speaking to *Sports Illustrated*, he remembered his reply: "That sounds terrible."

Instead, Carson trained his replacement. He and Stick watched video of Bison games. They watched video of teams the Bison would play.

Being a quarterback is about more than throwing the ball. It's also about leading. Wentz was a fifth-year senior. He'd had five years to learn how to lead. Now he had less than a week to get a freshman ready to be the Bison starting quarterback and take over the leadership role.

The Bison had five games left in the regular season. To reach the playoffs they could only lose one. The time Carson had spent with Stick paid off. The Bison won all five games. They made the playoffs. They weren't done. They won three more games in the playoffs.

For the national championship in January, the Bison faced the Jacksonville State Gamecocks. The day before the game, head coach Chris Klieman made an announcement. Carson would return as starting quarterback.

Carson knew he might hurt his wrist again. He might play badly because of his long layoff. Either outcome could harm his chance to play in the NFL.

The game wasn't close. Carson threw for 197 yards. He ran for 79. His team won, 37-10.

Soon afterward, he was in Los Angeles. He began working out with Ryan Lindley, a pro quarterback. Lindley would help him get ready for the Combine. Southern California was a big change for Carson. He'd learned to play football on a frozen field. During the winter his helmet was often covered in ice.

Carson Wentz (11) and quarterback Easton Stick (12) of the North Dakota State Bison celebrate with fans after defeating the Iowa State Cyclones 34-14 on August 30, 2014.

2 Competing

Carson James Wentz was born on December 30, 1992. His dad Doug had been a college football player. Now he works as a loan officer. Carson's mom Cathy Anhalt works for the American Heart Association.

As a youngster, Carson had a lot of energy. Sometimes it got him in trouble. Sometimes it drove his mom crazy.

She remembered what Carson was like growing up. "He has been a challenge since day one," Cathy told the website I Love to Watch You Play. "He always had to be busy doing something."

After a while she accepted it. It helped that he found an outlet. He started playing sports. He didn't just play one or two. He played six! Besides football, he liked baseball, basketball, hockey, golf, and soccer.

He also did well in school. He made the honor roll in high school. No matter what he did, only one thing mattered. "If he wasn't the best, he wasn't good enough," his mom added. The tough thing for Carson was that he wasn't even the best in his family. His brother Zach was. Zach was three years older.

Carson Wentz arrives at the 2016 NFL Draft, accompanied by his mother Cathy. The draft was held in Chicago.

"When I was a kid, I didn't necessarily dream about winning Super Bowls. . . . I wanted to beat Zach," Carson wrote in *The Players Tribune*. "Baseball, football, checkers, number of plates consumed at a buffet—it did not matter what we were doing, everything was a competition."

The family had moved to Bismarck, North Dakota when Carson was still a toddler. It is a place with brutal winters. The first snow usually hits around Halloween. The last snow of the season is in April.

Like Carson, journalist Brandon Anderson grew up in North Dakota. He wrote in *The Cauldron* that "Several times each winter, school gets cancelled because there's a blizzard or because it's literally too cold to go outside. And do you know what everyone does when that happens? All the boys in the neighborhood go outside, anyway. And they play

> *The family had moved to Bismarck, North Dakota when Carson was still a toddler. It is a place with brutal winters.*

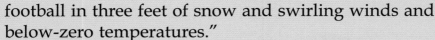

football in three feet of snow and swirling winds and below-zero temperatures."

Carson Wentz was one of those boys. For him, football wasn't just a game. It was a way to deal with some hard times. Before he was in elementary school, his parents divorced. His mother remarried. She and Kevin Anhalt had a son, Luke. Carson was nine when he became the middle kid.

He shared his brother's and father's love for football. When Carson was in fifth grade, he joined the Bismarck Youth Football League. In 2013, the league's director Lance Olson told the *Bismarck Tribune*, "I'm glad that we got to coach guys like [Major League Baseball player] Dalton Feeney or Carson Wentz, but those guys would have been superstars regardless."

Carson usually carried the ball. He later wrote that he was an "everyone-knows-where-the-ball-is-going" running back. It didn't make him easier to tackle. As he admitted in *The Player's Tribune*, "contact was always my favorite part of the game. . . . It was kind of funny, honestly. I was this crazy, string-bean

> *Carson Wentz was one of those boys. For him, football wasn't just a game.*

kid trying to truck kids into the end zone. And a lot of the time, I did."

His friends, teammates, and coaches all called him "humble" and "likeable" when they spoke with reporter Josh Paunil. They also remembered something else. He really, really hated to lose. Sometimes when he lost a game in middle school he would cry afterward.

Although Carson played sports with Kam Wingenbach in elementary school, they didn't become friends until seventh grade. They met while they were building robots for Tech Ed. Kam told barstoolsports.com that he remembers getting "an A and having the coolest robot in the class thanks to his [Carson's] outstanding leadership."

Carson hoped to demonstrate leadership with sports as well. He'd written down his dream of being a pro football player when he was just in second grade. There was one problem. He'd have to grow a whole lot. As a high school freshman, Carson was short and skinny. Some people thought that he might have been too small to play football. But when he tried out for the Century High School Patriots, the coaches knew he had something to offer. Football was a family tradition.

3 *Overshadowed*

Carson had just scored a touchdown. In the stands, Century High School fans cheered. Carson waited to hear his name called over the public address system. Then he heard it. The announcer called him "Zach."

Carson was used to people getting his name wrong. Sometimes local papers also mistook him for Zach. When Carson started high school, his brother was one of the best football players it had ever seen. In 2007, Zach set Century's single-season school passing record. He set records in baseball too. Meanwhile, Carson was still short and skinny. "I wasn't much to look at. I came in at 5'8" and about 125 pounds (depending on what I ate for lunch that day)," he wrote in *The Players Tribune*. He admitted that one of the biggest things he prayed for was to be over six feet. It was different for Zach. He was over six feet tall as a freshman. "Zach grew into his body earlier," the school's head football coach, Ron Wingenbach, told NBC Sports.

Zach's size meant he was a starting quarterback when his younger brother was playing whatever position coaches would give him. "I always thought the skill-set was there, but I didn't know what level or what

> **Zach's size meant he was a starting quarterback when his younger brother was playing whatever position coaches would give him.**

sport," Zach told the *Bismarck Tribune*. "He [Carson] was always a fairly high-strung guy, and I was more patient, so baseball was more for me. Carson likes to be on the go-go and he blossomed into the football kid."

Carson wasn't the biggest player. But he was usually the most determined. Kam Wingenbach remembered Carson visiting him at the golf course where he worked. He tried hitting the ball a few times, but didn't do very well. He returned a few days later with brand-new clubs. Every day he practiced. Finally, he hit a ball that soared 100 yards past the one Kam hit. "Most competitive guy I've ever met," Kam told *Philadelphia Magazine*. "It was kind of annoying. He always had to be the best at everything he did."

In 2010, Carson was a senior. The day basketball tryouts

began, coach Darrin Mattern bumped into Carson. He joked that he'd like to see him try basketball. Carson hadn't played in years. He still made the team. Mattern believes Carson was a big reason the Patriots went to the state championship.

The school's baseball coach and teammates remember Carson as a talented pitcher who

The school's baseball coach and teammates remember Carson as a talented pitcher who eventually decided to save his arm.

eventually decided to save his arm. He realized it was affecting football. He switched to third base and hit close to .500 as a senior. Unfortunately, playing baseball nearly ended his college football dreams before they started.

Tom Keller remembered Carson in high school. His friend had one big problem. He wanted to "get out from the shadow of his brother, because I know growing up he just hated when he was 'Zach's brother,'" Keller told Josh Paunil. By the time Carson was a junior, he had his chance.

His prayer to be over six feet tall had been answered. At 6-foot-5 and 235 pounds, he was even bigger than his older brother. Carson had a chance to be the Patriots' starting quarterback. Then during a

> *His prayer to be over six feet tall had been answered. At 6-foot-5 and 235 pounds, he was even bigger than his older brother.*

baseball game, he injured his right shoulder.

"His junior year is when we thought he was ready to make a big step," Wingenbach told the *Bucks County Herald*. "And he got hurt. It was kind of a lost season,"

But Carson didn't want to sit on the bench all season. He asked Wingenbach to let him play receiver. The coach was proud of Carson. Instead of sulking or giving up, he wanted to help the team. Near the end of the season, he got some playing time. Out of 25 years coaching the team, Wingenbach says his favorite times were when he had one of the Wentz brothers. "You wish you could [copy] them," he told the *Bismarck Tribune*. "It would make coaching a lot easier."

As a senior, Carson became the starting quarterback. He led the team to the playoffs. They faced Fargo. "Man, we wanted to beat those guys," Carson wrote in *The Player's Tribune*. "I really thought we had them, but they ended up scoring a touchdown with six seconds left in the game to go ahead by one. That's still the most heartbreaking loss of my life."

Carson warms up before a game so he will be ready to go full-speed when it starts.

Along with helping his team reach the playoffs, Carson spent most of the season waiting to hear from college teams. He hoped to get a scholarship from a Division I school. In the late fall, schools like Southern Illinois, South Dakota State, Central Michigan, and North Dakota State started asking about him. "Even then, it was lukewarm," coach Wingenbach told the *Bismarck Tribune*.

Every year, 247Sports rates high school football players. The best ones get a 101-110. Those are players that are very rare. The next level is "five-star" players. They earn a score of 98-100. The lowest is below 79. Even these players might be able to play in Division I.

What was Carson's ranking? He didn't get one. He was listed as 2,628th in the country. Still, he was ranked 7th in North Dakota.

Finally, North Dakota State University offered a scholarship. Carson signed a letter promising to play for them. He ended his senior year on a high note. He was valedictorian. That means he had the best grades in his class. His lowest grade was an A-minus.

Carson joined the Bison as a redshirt freshman. Doing this would allow him to be on the team for five years instead of four. He could practice. But he couldn't play.

After spending a game sitting on the bench, sometimes he'd call his friend Meyer Bohn. Bohn told *Philadelphia Magazine* about their talks. "I'm just so frustrated," Bohn remembered Wentz saying. "Having to sit back here, I know I can compete. I know I can do that job."

During high school, Carson had waited. He didn't get to be the starting quarterback for three years. At North Dakota State he had the same problem. Their quarterback, Brock Jensen, won more games than any other quarterback in FCS history. As a starter he had a 47–5 record. He won three FCS championships. Some people wondered why Carson didn't choose a school that needed a quarterback right away. He did his best to make the most of it.

During practices, he got to act as quarterback for the next team the Bison would face. The Bison defense was considered one of the best in the FCS Subdivision. Then-defensive coordinator Chris Klieman told

> **Carson found other ways to deal with his unhappiness.**

reporters the toughest quarterback his men faced all year was Carson, even though he was just a redshirt freshman.

Carson found other ways to deal with his unhappiness. He'd gotten into hunting in high school. In college he often went into the wilderness with a bow and arrow or a 12-gauge shotgun. He was usually joined by Henley, his golden retriever.

Back at school, he maintained an A average as a health and physical education major. He trained in the gym. And he reviewed game videos. He was so dedicated that many of his teammates thought he should be captain. A few even thought he was better than Jensen. But he wouldn't get a chance to be starting quarterback until his junior year, after Jensen graduated.

Carson scrambles under pressure from linebacker Jevohn Miller of the Iowa State Cyclones. In his first game as starter, Carson led his team to a 34–14 win.

During Bison home games, the Fargodome swells with some 19,000 screaming fans. The lights go down. Loud rock music blasts from the speakers. Players run through an inflatable helmet. It was a ritual Carson Wentz loved. During the 2014 season, it became even more meaningful. He was now the starting quarterback.

By then, he'd had a bit of playing time as the backup quarterback. In one game in his first season, he completed all eight of his passes. The next year he played in 11 games.

Some people worried he'd be a poor replacement for Jensen. Carson didn't throw a touchdown pass in his first two games. Two of his passes were intercepted. Yet the Bison still won. After winning the next two games, he told *USA Today*, "I've always been confident in my abilities and

Carson hugs coach Chris Klieman during their win against the Jacksonville State Gamecocks at the FCS Championship.

have known what I can do. It's been great to finally get out there and show it these four games."

Any doubt was erased by the end of the season. The Bison lost one game. He took them to the playoffs and then the national championship.

Carson drops back to pass during the 2016 Reese's Senior Bowl. The game highlights the country's best seniors.

By then, many people thought that Carson showed pro-level skills. During three of the four playoff games that season, he led the team to come-from-behind victories "Like it was no big deal," Klieman—now the head coach—told *Sports Illustrated*.

Against South Dakota State in the second round, Carson led the Bison on a late 76-yard drive. His final play was a 12-yard touchdown pass. "I can still see the play, and it's one of my favorite plays," quarterbacks coach Randy Hedberg told writer Josh Paunil. "He was so poised on the play fake, and he threw a strike into the corner of the end zone. There was only one place he could throw it for a completion, and he was right on the money."

His broken wrist caused him to miss much of the 2015 season, but his performance in the title game showed that he was back at full strength. So did the Combine. Carson was in the top three among quarterbacks in the 40-yard dash, the long jump, and the three-cone drill. A scout taking a look at Carson told a reporter that, "I see everything. Arm strength. Accuracy. Toughness. Athletic ability. Smart. Great kid," according to NFL.com. "He could be really good. He's the best runner, he's the best athlete. He is off the charts."

While he waited for the NFL Draft, Carson lived in a house with five roommates. He slept in the living room, sharing his air mattress with Henley. "I showed my agent [the place] a few weeks ago," he told *Sports Illustrated*. The agent would help him get the best deal when he was chosen. The agent told him, "No one's life is about to change more than yours." He was right.

Carson's performance in college and the Combine attracted the attention of the Philadelphia Eagles. The team traded five draft choices to the Cleveland Browns. That gave them Cleveland's number two spot in the draft. No other quarterback in the FCS had ever been drafted as high. Carson would receive

Carson holds up a jersey with NFL Commissioner Roger Goodell after being picked #2 overall by the Philadelphia Eagles.

$26 million as part of a four-year contract. Over $17 million would be a signing bonus.

Later that year, Carson graduated from college. He earned all As and a 4.0 grade point average.

The Winning Season

5

Philadelphia Eagles fans were tired of waiting. So was Carson. In 2015, the team had a 7-9 record. With a new coach and a new quarterback, fans looked forward to the 2016 season. Over the summer, Wentz wondered if he would once again be waiting on the bench. The team planned to use his first year for him to learn plays and prepare to lead. Instead, on September 3, the Eagles traded starting quarterback Sam Bradford to the Minnesota Vikings. That meant Carson wouldn't have to wait. He began the season as the starter.

He also began breaking records. He won his first game on September 11th. Throwing two touchdowns, Carson was named the Rookie of the Week. His next week was just as good. Once again, the Eagles won. In over 40 years, no other rookie quarterback had won his first two games without throwing an interception.

Carson started all 16 games. He completed 379 passes. That was an NFL record for a rookie. Unfortunately, the team finished the season with the same record as the year before.

The 2017 season proved to Eagles fans that the money spent for their new quarterback was worth it.

Carson walks off the field after his first game as a starter. The Eagles defeated the Cleveland Browns 29–10. Carson completed 22 passes for 278 yards and two touchdowns.

The team won 10 of its first 11 games. In October, Carson threw more touchdown passes in a month than any other Eagles quarterback. Many people believed he would be named the Most Valuable Player in the NFL at the end of the season. Fans hoped he'd take the team all the way to the Super Bowl.

Carson enjoyed the fans' praise. Yet he stayed focused. He admitted to *Philadelphia Magazine* that, "My faith helps me never get too high, never get too low about things, such as when I broke my wrist or when we lose. I believe there's a plan." He was not alone in his new home. He'd brought his dog Henley with him. "I love dogs and being around them," Carson

> **Carson enjoyed the fans' praise. Yet he stayed focused.**

Carson throws one of his four touchdown passes against the Denver Broncos on November 5, 2017. The Eagles won 51–23.

told Jeff Karr at 247Sports. "It's a fun process getting away from everything else going on in life and just getting to spend time with them."

Unfortunately, Carson suffered a severe knee injury late in the season. Many people wrote off the Eagles even though their 13–3 season record was the best in the National Football Conference of the NFL. Nick Foles took over for Carson and directed the Eagles to a thrilling 41–33 victory over the New England Patriots in Super Bowl LII. It was the team's first Super Bowl win.

Even though Carson wasn't on the field, he still played an important role in the triumph. "Carson instilled a confidence, a swagger and a belief," Eagles offensive coordinator Frank Reich told *The New York Times*. "That's the kind of leader and player he is."

Philadelphia fans look forward to many more years of Carson's leadership and brilliant performances.

Nick Foles (left) and Carson celebrate following the Eagles' victory over the New England Patriots in Super Bowl LII on February 4, 2018.

1992 Carson James Wentz is born on December 30, 1992 in Raleigh, North Carolina to Doug and Cathy Wentz.

1996 The Wentz family moves to Bismarck, North Dakota.

2003 Begins playing football with the Bismarck Youth Football League.

2008 Carson joins the Century High School football team.

2009 He plays baseball for Century High School, but an injury keeps him from playing football.

2010 Starts at quarterback and defensive back.

2011 Carson graduates as valedictorian from Century High School; he redshirts for the North Dakota State Bison.

2012 Plays in his first collegiate game in September.

2014 In his first year as starting quarterback, he leads the Bison to a 15-1 record and the national championship.

2015 He leads the Bison to another national championship despite missing eight games with a broken wrist.

2016 He is drafted by the Philadelphia Eagles and begins the season as the starting quarterback.

2017 He leads the Eagles to a winning season but is injured shortly before the Super Bowl.

CAREER STATS

Year	Team	PA	PC	Y	TD
2012	North Dakota State	16	12	144	2
2013	North Dakota State	30	22	209	1
2014	North Dakota State	358	228	3,111	25
2015	North Dakota State	208	130	1,651	17
2016	Philadelphia Eagles	607	379	3,782	16
2017	Philadelphia Eagles	440	265	3,296	33

Legend: PA = passes attempted; PC= passes completed; Y = Yardage; TD = touchdowns

FIND OUT MORE

Books

Editors of Sports Illustrated Kids. *Football: Then to WOW!* New York:
    Sports Illustrated, 2014.

Gramling, Gary. *The Football Fanbook: Everything You Need to Become a
    Gridiron Know-it-All.* New York: Sports Illustrated, 2017.

On the Internet

Carson Wentz: Philadelphia Eagles
    http://www.nfl.com/player/carsonwentz/2555259/profile

FCS Stats
    http://www.fcs.football/fcsfront.asp

WORKS CONSULTED

Periodicals

Andrews, Malika. "For Eagles' Carson Wentz, an Imperfect
    Super Bowl Moment. *The New York Times*, February 5, 2018.
    https://www.nytimes.com/2018/02/05/sports/football/carson-
    wentz-eagles-super-bowl.html

Babiarz, Lou. "BMFL Celebrates 40 Years of Teaching Football."
    Bismarck Tribune, November 12, 2013. http://bismarcktribune.
    com/sports/local/bmfl-celebrates-years-of-teaching-football/
    article_785adb48-4c14-11e3-9690-0019bb2963f4.html

Bishop, Greg. "Inside the Low-profile Life of Top QB Prospect Carson
    Wentz." *Sports Illustrated*, April 18, 2016. https://www.si.com/
    nfl/2016/04/27/nfl-draft-2016-carson-wentz-north-dakota-state

Bowen, Les. "Brother, Sister-in-Law Coming to Philly to Help Wentz
    Settle In." *The [Philadelphia] Inquirer*, May 1, 2016. http://www.
    philly.com/philly/columnists/les_bowen/20160501_Brother__
    sister-in-law_coming_to_Philly_to_help_Wentz_settle_in.html

Garry, Mick. "Unbelievable: USD Stuns No. 2 North Dakota State." *Argus Leader*, October 17, 2015. http://www.argusleader.com/ story/sports/college/university-of-south-dakota/2015/10/17/ unbelievable-coyotes-stun-no-3-ndsu/74050358/

Leypoldt, Don. "The Cultivation of Carson Wentz: A Conversation with Ron Wingenbach." *Bucks County Herald*.

"New Starting Quarterback Comes Out Strong." *USA Today*, October 1, 2014. https://www.usatoday.com/story/sports/ ncaaf/2014/10/01/new-starting-quarterback-at-ndsu-comes-out-strong/16553951/

Nicholson, Blake and Regina Garcia Cano. "NDSU starting QB Wentz out 6-8 Weeks with Broken Wrist." *The San Diego Union-Tribune*, October 20, 2015. http://www.sandiegouniontribune.com/sdut-ndsu-starting-quarterback-carson-wentz-suffers-2015oct20-story. html

Paunil, Josh. "Carson Wentz in Pursuit of Perfection." *Philadelphia Magazine*, May 12, 2016. http://www.phillymag.com/ birds247/2016/05/12/carson-wentz-chasing-perfection-philadelphia-eagles/

Vrentas, Jenny. "Everyone Believes in Carson Wentz Now." *Sports Illustrated*, October 24, 2017.https://www.si.com/ nfl/2017/10/24/carson-wentz-eagles-redskins

Zangaro, Dave. "Close Relationship with Brother Zach Helped Mold Carson Wentz." *NBC Sports*, April 30, 2016.

Web Sites

"247 Rating Explanation" 247Sports, July 20, 2012. https://247sports. com/Article/247Rating-Explanation-81574

Anderson, Brandon. "The Truth About Carson Wentz From a North Dakota Insider." *The Cauldron*, April 29, 2016. https://the-cauldron.com/carson-wentz-fact-or-fiction-a5a6a316c878

"Carson Wentz Kept Nine Dogs in His House Last September." 247Sports, July 19, 2017. https://247sports.com/nfl/philadelphia-eagles/Bolt/Carson-Wentz-kept-nine-dogs-in-his-house-last-December-104012393

"Carson Wentz Varsity Football." Max Preps, April 2016.
http://www.maxpreps.com/athlete/carson-wentz/
RZJbYPTtEeKZ5AAmVebBJg/default.htm

Erdman, Jon. "When the First Snow of the Season Typically Falls."
weather.com, September 30, 2017. https://weather.com/storms/
winter/news/first-snow-average-date

Ferrone, Adam. "Exclusive Interview With Carson Wentz's
Childhood Best Friend," barstoolsports.com, September 19, 2016.
https://www.barstoolsports.com/philadelphia/exclusive-
interview-with-carson-wentzs-childhood-best-friend-who-was-
behind-the-trick-shot-video/

Flanagan, Alex. "My Son, Carson Wentz, Is Going Pro." I Love to
Watch You Play, April 28, 2016. https://ilovetowatchyouplay.
com/2016/04/28/my-son-is-going-pro-tonight/

Kerr, Jeff. "Eagles QB Carson Wentz when He was in High School."
CBS Sports, February 1, 2017. https://www.cbssports.com/nfl/
news/eagles-qb-carson-wentz-when-he-was-in-high-school/

"NFL Scouting Combine." http://www.nflcombine.net

Panterno, Joe. "FCS Championship 2016: NDSU vs. Jacksonville
State Score and Twitter Reaction." 247Sports, January 9, 2016.
http://bleacherreport.com/articles/2606393-fcs-championship-
2016-ndsu-vs-jacksonville-state-score-and-twitter-reaction

Sessier, Marc. "Philadelphia Eagles Draft Carson Wentz." NFL.com,
April 29, 2016.

Wentz, Carson. "How We Play Football in North Dakota." Players
Tribune, April 25, 2016. https://www.theplayerstribune.com/
carson-wentz-north-dakota-state-nfl-draft/